P9-CNB-879

WITHDRAWN

Fact Finders®

RACE FOR HISTORY

WHO REALLY CREATED DEMOCRACY?

by Amie Jane Leavitt

Fitchburg Public Library
5530 Lacy Road
Fitchburg, WI 53711

CAPSTONE PRESS
a capstone imprint

Fact Finders are published by Capstone Press,
151 Good Counsel Drive, P.O. Box 669, Mankato, Minnesota 56002.
www.capstonepub.com

Copyright © 2011 by Capstone Press, a Capstone imprint.
All rights reserved.
No part of this publication may be reproduced in whole or in part, or stored in a retrieval system,
or transmitted in any form or by any means, electronic, mechanical, photocopying, recording,
or otherwise, without written permission of the publisher.
For information regarding permission, write to Capstone Press,
151 Good Counsel Drive, P.O. Box 669, Dept. R, Mankato, Minnesota 56002.

 Books published by Capstone Press are manufactured with paper
containing at least 10 percent post-consumer waste.

Library of Congress Cataloging-in-Publication Data
Leavitt, Amie Jane.
Who really created democracy? / by Amie Jane Leavitt.
p. cm.—(Fact finders. Race for history)
Includes bibliographical references and index.
Summary: "Follows the stories of the ancient Greeks in Athens and the American colonists
as they struggle to create democracies"—Provided by publisher.
ISBN 978-1-4296-3343-7 (library binding)
ISBN 978-1-4296-6246-8 (paperback)
1. Democracy—History—Juvenile literature. I. Title. II. Series.
JC423.L388 2011
321.8—dc22   2010026028

Editorial Credits
Jennifer Besel, editor; Alison Thiele, series designer; Bobbie Nuytten, book designer;
    Wanda Winch, media researcher; Eric Manske, production specialist

Photo Credits
The Bridgeman Art Library International: Peter Newark American Pictures/Private Collection, 9 (left), Photo
©Whiteford & Hughes, London, UK/©DACS/Private Collection/Rochegrosse, Georges Marie, 6, The Stapleton
Collection/Private Collection/Margaret Dovaston, cover (top left), 27, The Stapleton Collection/Private Collection/
Walter Crane, 13; Capstone: Terry Riley, 5 (bottom); Corbis: Bettmann, 10; Courtesy of Army Art Collection, U.S.
Army Center of Military History, 21; Getty Images Inc.: The Bridgeman Art Library/Courtesy of the Council,
National Army Museum/William Barnes Wollen, 15, MPI, 25; The Granger Collection, New York, 23; Library of
Congress, Prints and Photographs Division, 9 (right); Nova Development Corporation, 28-29 (all); Shutterstock: U.P.
images (banner design) SuperStock Inc.: SuperStock, cover (bottom), 5 (top), 16, 17; Wikipedia, cover (top right), 19

**Capstone Press thanks Professor Michael J. G. Cain, director of the Center for the Study of Democracy
and chairman of the Political Science Department at St. Mary's College of Maryland, for his assistance
with this book.**

Printed in the United States of America in Stevens Point, Wisconsin.
092010   005934WZS11

TABLE OF CONTENTS

THE RACE. 4

Chapter 1 *TROUBLE'S BREWING* 6
Chapter 2 *BIG DECISIONS*. 10
Chapter 3 *BATTLING IT OUT* 18
Chapter 4 *MAKING DEMOCRACIES* 22

THE WINNER 26

TIMELINE 28
GLOSSARY 30
READ MORE 31
INTERNET SITES. 31
INDEX 32

THE RACE

For thousands of years, people have been organizing into cities and countries. Their governments create rules to follow. But often wealthy people control how the countries are run. The poor have little or no power in the government.

In answer to this problem, democracy was born. In a democracy, people—rich and poor—make laws together. They also choose their own leaders. But where did this idea come from? Who created democracy? The race to democracy is long and difficult. The players are divided by centuries. But only one can be the winner. Who will it be?

AMERICAN COLONISTS

These people have settled in the 13 American colonies. By the 1770s, many colonists have lived in America their entire lives. But Great Britain still controls the colonies. Many colonists don't believe Great Britain treats America fairly.

ANCIENT GREEKS IN ATHENS

These people live in Athens in the fifth and fourth centuries BC. Most of the citizens are poor farmers who owe debts to the wealthy rulers of their city. They are frustrated and looking for change.

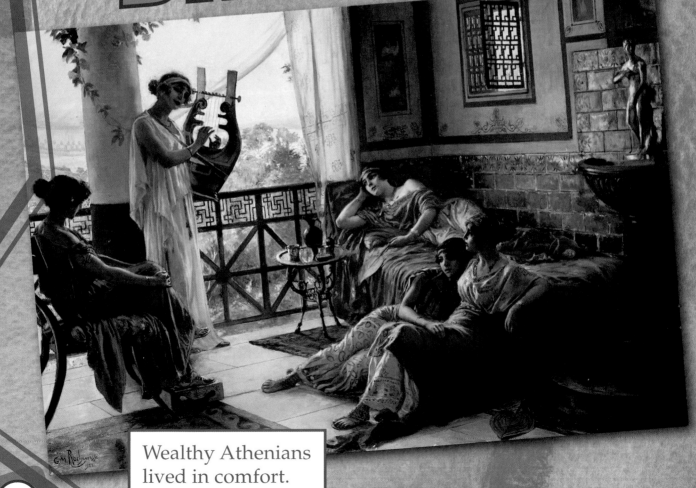

CHAPTER ONE
TROUBLE'S BREWING

Wealthy Athenians lived in comfort.

Life in Athens

Athens in 630 BC is a great city for the rich. The wealthy relax in comfortable homes. They own large plots of land and eat delicious food. And they make all of the laws for everyone else.

Only the rich are part of the **oligarchy** that rules Athens. Most Athenians are poor and struggle to grow crops on their tiny farms. They have to borrow money to buy food and pay taxes. They also have no say in Athen's laws.

The oligarchy's laws are very strict. If people can't pay their debts, they must sell family members into slavery. Families all over Athens are being separated this way. The poor are angry and frustrated.

At first, people just talk about their unhappiness. But soon, the talking grows to shouting. Then it grows to action. The poor begin to fight against wealthy rulers. Athens is no longer a peaceful city.

The poor outnumber the rich. The wealthy lawmakers know they can't fight the masses. But Athens is heading straight for a civil war. The rulers have to make changes to the government quickly. Is there any way to bring peace?

RACE FACT Athens was a city-state. City-states had their own armies, governments, and cultures. There were more than 100 city-states in ancient Greece.

oligarchy: a government ruled by only a few people

Life in the Colonies

It's 1773. Times are tough in the 13 American colonies. King George III lives across the ocean in Great Britain. But his presence is felt every day. He put taxes on things such as stamps and now tea. He has put colonists in prison without fair trials.

The colonists are most angry because they don't have any power in government. In Great Britain, citizens don't get to choose the king. But at least they get to vote for the people in **Parliament**. The colonists are British citizens too. But they don't get to vote.

Anger in the colonies begins to bubble over. If the colonists don't have a vote, why should they follow the laws? One night **patriots** storm merchant ships in Boston. They dump barrels of tea into the harbor. They won't drink the king's tea, and they won't pay tax on it either!

The king is furious. He makes even harsher laws. The colonists begin to whisper plans for war. The situation is quickly spinning out of control.

Parliament: the group of people who have been elected to make the laws in England

patriot: an American who disagreed with British rule

the Boston Tea Party

King George III

CHAPTER TWO
BIG DECISIONS

Solon (left) telling
people about his laws

Changing the Rule of Athens

The unrest in Athens is also spinning out of control. The wealthy rulers need to find a way to calm the city. They quickly make a plan. In 594 BC, they turn the government over to an **aristocrat** named Solon. They hope he can bring peace to Athens.

Solon was born to a powerful family. But he's also lived the life of a common person. He spent many years working as a trader. For this reason, the common people seem to like him.

Members of the oligarchy know it's dangerous to give all the power to one person. The poor people know it too. If Solon wants, he can make himself king and create whatever laws he wants.

RACE FACT

Solon liked to write poetry. Much of what historians know about Solon comes from his poems.

aristocrat: a member of a group of people thought to be the best in some way, usually based on their wealth

But Solon doesn't want to abuse his power. He loves Athens and wants to settle the trouble. First, Solon changes the debtors' laws. No longer will Athenians have to sell family members to pay debts. He even brings back people who were sold as slaves.

The people are excited about this change. But the poor still have no voice in the government. If Solon wants, he can change the law back anytime.

Then Solon starts to rearrange the government and society. He divides citizens into four classes based on how much their farms produce. People can move into a higher class by growing more food. The people in the top three classes are allowed to run for government office. In this new system, the aristocrats no longer control everything.

The common people like what Solon is doing. But the lowest class still can't be part of the government. And they're still struggling to feed their families and pay debts to the aristocrats. Solon's changes just aren't enough.

The aristocrats aren't happy either. They don't like that the lower classes have some power now. A negative buzz can be heard in Athens. No one is really happy. Can Solon's new government survive?

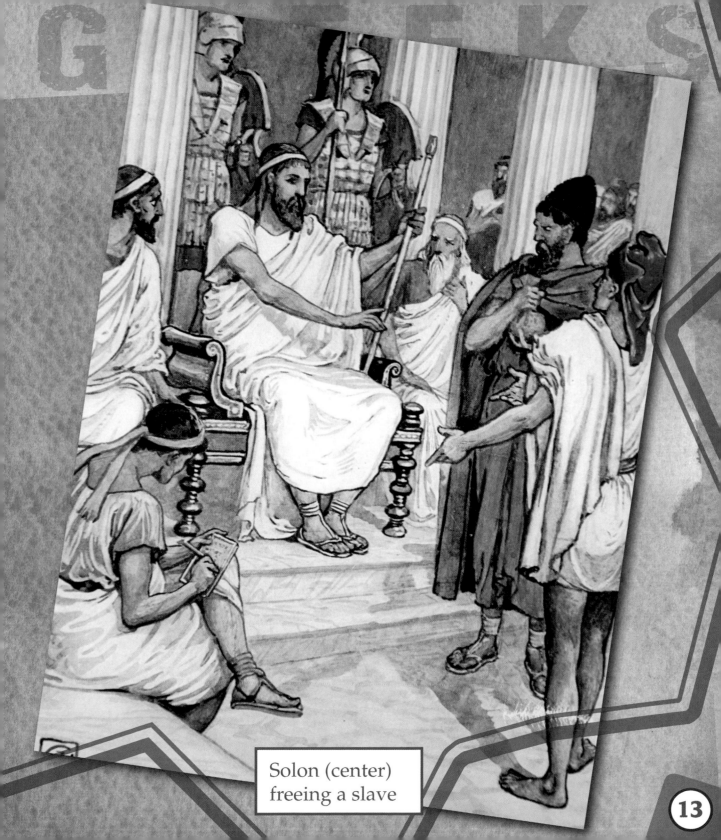

Solon (center)
freeing a slave

The Colonists Go to War

The American colonists continue to struggle with their government. The patriots hate Britain's unfair treatment of the colonies. But what can they do? After the Tea Party, Parliament closed Boston harbor. British soldiers now march through the colonies. And the king just signed a bill that forces colonists to house and feed those soldiers.

Patriot leaders meet in Philadelphia in September 1774. Leaders at the Continental Congress discuss what should be done. Finally, they decide the colonies will stop all trade with Great Britain. They also write a letter to the king. They ask for fair treatment and a voice in the government.

The patriots' efforts only make the king and Parliament more angry. In April 1775, the king orders British troops to destroy the colonists' storage of weapons. Word of the plan leaks out. The patriots prepare to fight.

The British army marches toward Lexington, Massachusetts. When the soldiers arrive, a small band of patriots is waiting. A British officer orders the patriots to drop their weapons and leave. The Americans face an army of hundreds of trained soldiers. They have no choice but to back down. They turn to go, but they won't leave their guns. Suddenly, a gunshot rings out. A British officer orders his troops to fire. The patriots fire back. It's war!

The patriots fought the British at the Battle of Lexington on April 19, 1775.

RACE FACT

Historians don't know which side fired the first shot that started the Revolutionary War.

Jefferson (standing) worked with other patriots like Benjamin Franklin (left) and John Adams (center) on the declaration.

In June 1776, patriot leaders ask Thomas Jefferson to write a **declaration.** They want to tell the world that they are fighting this war to be independent from Great Britain. In the document, Jefferson lists the ways the king has wronged the colonists. The king has refused to give them a say in the government. He has made them pay unfair taxes. He hasn't given the colonists fair trials. Jefferson writes that the colonists will no longer take this unjust treatment.

The document is presented to the patriot leaders on July 4, 1776. Fifty-six men sign their names to the Declaration of Independence. By doing so, they are committing **treason** against Great Britain. The king could have them killed for this act. Winning the war is now life or death for the colonists.

RACE FACT

Two future presidents signed the declaration—John Adams and Thomas Jefferson.

signing the Declaration of Independence

declaration: a public announcement

treason: the crime of betraying your country or government

CHAPTER THREE

BATTLING IT OUT

Fighting in Athens

The situation has grown extremely dangerous in Athens. People battle for control of the city. Solon's government cannot survive. In 561 BC a rich, powerful man named Peisistratus brings soldiers to Athens. He takes control of the government. Solon is old and weak. He warns that Peisistratus is a **tyrant**. But Peisistratus tells the people he was chosen by the god Athena. They agree to let him rule.

Peisistratus does many good things for Athens. He increases trade to the city. He also has channels built to bring water to Athens. But the people have no control over what Peisistratus does. He makes all the laws and rules the government.

tyrant: someone who rules in a cruel way

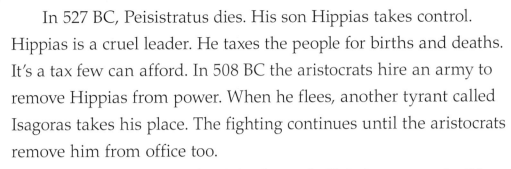

In 527 BC, Peisistratus dies. His son Hippias takes control. Hippias is a cruel leader. He taxes the people for births and deaths. It's a tax few can afford. In 508 BC the aristocrats hire an army to remove Hippias from power. When he flees, another tyrant called Isagoras takes his place. The fighting continues until the aristocrats remove him from office too.

Now it is 507 BC. Athen's leaders ask Cleisthenes to rebuild the government. Cleisthenes had helped defeat Hippias, and he has ideas for a new government. The people hope Cleisthenes' new government will give them a say in how they're ruled. But there is a chance that their new ruler will be another terrible tyrant.

Cleisthenes

Fighting in the Colonies

American colonists know what a tyrant's rule is like. And they are willing to fight against it. But winning the war against King George III is going to be hard—if not impossible. Most colonists are not trained soldiers. And they're fighting one of the best militaries in the world.

During the war, the Continental Congress forms a set of rules for the colonies to follow. The Articles of Confederation give individual states a lot of power. In fact it's almost like there are 13 different countries.

The Revolutionary War is a long, bloody war. Thousands of fighters lose their lives. Finally, on October 19, 1781, the ending scenes of the war unfold. Britain's General Charles Cornwallis surrenders to General George Washington. The impossible has just become possible. A ragtag army has defeated the most powerful nation in the world!

Now in 1787, the colonies are independent. But they are struggling to keep the new country together. Each state has its own laws and money. And the states are taxing citizens to pay huge war debts. Many people lose their land because they can't pay the taxes.

It's clear the Articles of Confederation aren't working. The Articles created a Congress for the country, but it can do very little. And the American people don't even vote for members of Congress. The state governments choose who will serve. This isn't what the colonists fought for. They want a government that is chosen by the people. Some leaders wonder, "Did the ancient Greeks have this much trouble?"

Battle at Guilford Courthouse

CHAPTER FOUR

MAKING DEMOCRACIES

An Athens Ruled by the People

The ancient Athenians have had their share of trouble. For more than 50 years, they've been ruled by tyrants. But Cleisthenes is no tyrant. In fact, he wants a government run by the people.

Cleisthenes' first action makes more free men citizens. Before this time, a man had to be born in the city to be a citizen. Now, those born in the countryside are citizens too. Then Cleisthenes allows all citizens to be members of the Assembly. The Assembly is the city's lawmaking body. Every citizen—rich and poor—gets a vote here.

Assembly meetings occur on a hill outside Athens every 10 days. Thousands come to listen to speakers debate laws, wars, and taxes. No laws are made in Athens unless they are approved by the Assembly.

RACE FACT

Women in ancient Athens were not considered citizens. They did not get to participate in the Assembly.

Cleisthenes also forms the Council of the Five Hundred to run the daily business of the city. Citizens draw **lots** to serve on the council. Being on the council gives citizens a chance to directly lead the government. Ideas for laws or taxes start in the council. Then the council brings ideas to the Assembly for a vote.

It has taken years for this day to come. But finally the people of Athens have what they fought for. They have a government ruled by the people!

People gave speeches to the Assembly about laws and taxes.

lot: an object a person picks randomly to be selected for something

A Democratic America

A government ruled by the people is also becoming a reality in America. In May 1787, state leaders meet in Philadelphia to discuss a new plan for the country. The men use their knowledge of the past to guide their future. They discuss Solon, Cleisthenes, and the government of ancient Athens. They review the Magna Carta, a document that forced British kings to follow laws.

The leaders debate many issues. After four long months, they finally come to an agreement. Their new government will share power between the national and state governments. It will also divide power between judicial, executive, and legislative branches.

The leaders also decide to give people a voice in their government. Citizens won't vote for every law. They will vote for leaders who make the laws. If the people don't like how leaders act, they can vote them out.

Finally, the people have what they fought for. The United States is officially ruled by the people!

The leaders wrote the Constitution of the United States to explain the new government.

RACE FACT

A democracy wasn't the only kind of government the leaders discussed. Some people wanted George Washington to be king.

THE WINNER

Both players overcame many hurdles in the race for democracy. But it was the people of ancient Greece who were the winners. In 507 BC, the people of Athens formed a government they called a democracy, or people power. Today we call their government a direct democracy. In direct democracies citizens vote directly for laws.

The patriots in America created a government run by the people too. However, they weren't the first to do so. The Americans actually studied Athen's ancient democracy when they designed their government. Unlike the ancient Greeks, the Americans didn't allow citizens to vote for every law. But they did allow them to vote for representatives who would make laws for them. This type of government is called a representative democracy.

Many other nations have followed in the footsteps of the Greeks and Americans. Today more than 100 nations have democratic governments. People in other countries are fighting for a say in their governments. If you look at it in that way, the race for democracy continues today.

The Assembly met in an area called the Pynx to listen to speakers and decide laws.

TIMELINE

630 BC The oligarchy rules in Athens, but the people are unhappy and begin to fight the rulers.

527 BC Hippias, Peisistratus' son, takes control of Athens.

507 BC Cleisthenes takes control of Athens. He creates the world's first democracy.

630 BC

561 BC Peisistratus takes over in Athens.

594 BC Solon comes to power in Athens.

508 BC Aristocrats and soldiers fight Hippias. Hippias flees, and Isagoras takes over. The fighting continues until Isagoras also flees.

OCTOBER 25, 1760 King George III takes the throne in Great Britain. Soon, colonists are frustrated with his rules and taxes.

SEPTEMBER 1774

The Continental Congress meets in Philadelphia. They write a letter to the king, asking for representation in the government.

Leaders from each state hold a Constitutional Convention. They form a representative democracy for the United States.

MAY 1787

JULY 4. 1776

Patriot leaders sign the Declaration of Independence.

AD 1787

APRIL 19. 1775

Patriot troops gather in Lexington to defend against approaching British soldiers. The first shots of the Revolutionary War are fired.

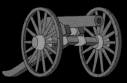

DECEMBER 16. 1773

OCTOBER 19. 1781

The British army surrenders. The Americans have won independence.

Patriots dump tea into Boston Harbor to protest the king's tea tax.

GLOSSARY

aristocrat (uh-RIS-tuh-krat)—a member of a group of people thought to be the best in some way, usually based on how much money they have; aristocrats are members of the highest social rank or nobility

declaration (de-kluh-RAY-shuhn)—a public announcement

lot (LOT)—an object a person draws randomly, such as a straw, to decide who will do or get something

oligarchy (OL-i-gahr-kee)—a government ruled by only a few people who are usually wealthy

Parliament (PAR-luh-muhnt)—the group of people who have been elected to make the laws in England

patriot (PAY-tree-uht)—an American colonist who disagreed with British rule of the American colonies

treason (TREE-zuhn)—the crime of being disloyal to your country or government

tyrant (TYE-ruhnt)—someone who rules other people in a cruel or unjust way

READ MORE

Hull, Robert. *Ancient Greece.* Exploring the Ancient World. New York: Gareth Stevens Pub., 2011.

O'Donnell, Liam. *Democracy.* Cartoon Nation. Mankato, Minn.: Capstone Press, 2008.

Price, Sean. *Designing America: The Constitutional Convention.* American History through Primary Sources. Chicago.: Raintree, 2008.

INTERNET SITES

FactHound offers a safe, fun way to find Internet sites related to this book. All of the sites on FactHound have been researched by our staff.

Here's all you do:

Visit www.facthound.com

Type in this code: 9781429633437

Check out projects, games and lots more at
www.capstonekids.com

INDEX

American Revolutionary War, 14, 15, 20
aristocrats, 11, 12, 19
Articles of Confederation, 20, 21
Assembly, 22, 23

Battle of Lexington, 14
Boston Tea Party, 8, 14

citizens, 5, 8, 22, 23, 24, 26
city-states, 7
Cleisthenes, 19, 22–23, 24
Constitutional Convention, 24
Continental Congress, 14, 20
Council of the Five Hundred, 23

debtors' laws, 7, 12
Declaration of Independence, 16–17
direct democracy, 26

George III, King, 8, 14, 16, 17, 20

Hippias, 19

Jefferson, Thomas, 16, 17

oligarchy, 7, 11

Parliament, 8, 14
patriots, 8, 14, 16–17, 26
Peisistratus, 18–19

representative democracy, 26

Solon, 11, 12, 18, 24

taxes, 7, 8, 16, 19, 20, 22, 23
treason, 17
tyrants, 18–19, 22

voting, 22, 23, 24, 26

Washington, George, 20, 25